Tommy and the Tornado

by Darleen Ramos
Illustrated by Anni Matsick

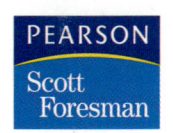

PEARSON
Scott Foresman

Editorial Offices: Glenview, Illinois • Parsippany, New Jersey • New York, New York
Sales Offices: Needham, Massachusetts • Duluth, Georgia • Glenview, Illinois
Coppell, Texas • Sacramento, California • Mesa, Arizona

Tommy lived on a farm in Oklahoma. He was a typical eleven-year-old boy. He liked to ride his bike, fish at the creek, and spend time with Tex, his loyal four-legged friend.

Most Saturdays were fun days, but this Saturday was going to be different. Tommy's parents had a wedding to attend, so they asked Christopher, Tommy's teen-aged brother, to watch him. Tommy enjoyed spending time with Christopher, but he didn't think his brother needed to take care of him.

"I don't need a babysitter," Tommy thought, "but at least I don't have to go to a wedding!"

---
typical: regular, usual

barn

corn field

The Oklahoma skies were blue and dotted with clouds as white as new snow. "What a great day to fish at the creek!" Tommy said. But Christopher was not in the mood to go fishing. Instead he said, "Let's go look for the old tools that Granddad left in the barn." Looking for Granddad's treasures sounded like a good idea to Tommy. The two boys ran to the barn. Tex followed, wagging his long tail.

Extend Language **Simile**

As white as new snow is a simile. Similes are used to compare two things that are different in some way.

Read other common similes below. Use each one in a new sentence.

- As strong as a bull
- As quiet as a mouse
- As soft as cotton
- As brave as a lion

Christopher slowly opened the squeaky door of the barn. Inside, it smelled like hay and old wood. The boys climbed the ladder to the hayloft of the barn. Tex stayed below. The hayloft was dark and dusty, so Tommy was not surprised when he stubbed his toe on an old trunk.

"Hey, what do you think is in here?" Tommy asked his older brother.

---

squeaky: noisy and shrill

Christopher carefully opened the trunk. It had several old quilts their grandmother had made and some old photographs. Tommy focused his attention on one photo.

"This picture must have been taken after the tornado ripped off the barn roof and sent it flying. I guess that's when they constructed the hiding hole."

When Tommy was a little boy, he called the storm cellar "the hiding hole." Christopher teased him about that, but now the entire family called it the hiding hole.

Tex started whining. Tommy thought he had trapped a mouse, but he saw that Tex was looking outside. His ears were down, and he seemed excited. Tommy opened the hay door to let in more light. The clouds had changed. The white fluffy clouds had disappeared. In their place were huge dark clouds that looked like they were boiling. The sky turned green. Then bugs started flying into the barn.

Most people who live in Oklahoma know the signs of a serious storm. Tommy and Christopher had learned about tornadoes in school. When a tornado is coming, the sky turns a strange green color, and many insects are in the air. There is often a strange stillness. Then, light rain or hail falls.

"Chris, I think we better go to the hiding hole. The sky looks pretty weird out there." Light rain started to fall. Tommy knew what was happening.

twister

corn stalks

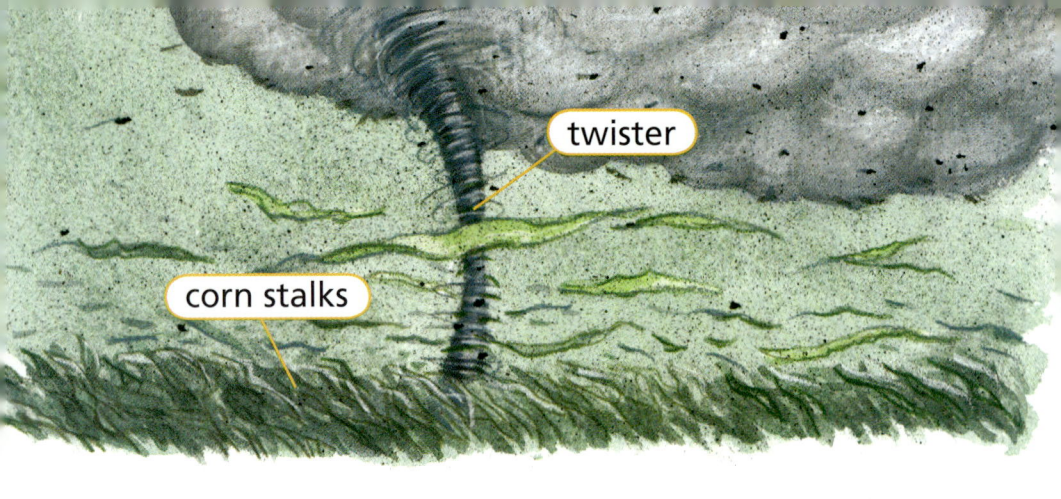

"Let's go!" he yelled and hurried down the ladder.

Tommy saw the frightening tornado in the distance. It was tearing up corn fields. It looked as though it was headed toward the old barn!

Christopher was running toward the barn door when he fell. "I hurt my ankle!" Christopher yelled. "You'll have to help me get to the cellar."

The noise of the tornado was thunderous, and Tommy could barely hear Christopher. Tommy was a resourceful boy, and he grabbed the quilts that had been tossed down by the wind.

Tommy shouted: "Cover up and stay low to the ground. Everything is flying all around! Lean on me! Let's go!"

Extend Language The Suffix -ous

The suffix –ous means "full of" or "having much."

Thunderous means "full of thunder."

Can you tell what *famous* means? The root word is *fame*.

How about *joyous* and *laborious*?

Clue: First, find out what the root word is, and what it means.

storm cellar

Christopher leaned on Tommy to support himself. The boys bent low and used the quilts for protection. Tommy could barely see where they were going, but Tex knew where they had to go. Tex led the boys to the storm cellar.

The tornado sounded like a train heading toward them. The wind was throwing corn stalks, branches, and dirt all around. Tommy opened the cellar door, and Tex quickly trotted down the stairs.

When all were inside the storm cellar, Tommy slammed the thick wooden door shut and turned on the battery-powered lantern his parents stored in the cellar. They could hear the wind blowing furiously above them.

Did You Know? Storm Cellars

- Many people who live in areas with tornadoes have storm cellars.
- Old storm cellars usually were dug in the ground outside of the home. The hole was framed with wood, and a heavy door was attached to the frame.
- Wooden steps lead down to the cellar.
- Some families stock their storm cellars with flashlights, batteries, blankets, and water.

Just as rapidly as it approached, the tornado passed by. Tommy gave Christopher his hand. "Let's see what kind of devastation this twister caused."

Tommy helped Christopher walk to the house. About an hour later, their parents returned home earlier than expected. They looked worried. "We tried calling you, but the tornado tore down many telephone lines. We wanted to make sure that everyone was safe," said the father.

"I was supposed to take care of Tommy, but he took care of me!" Christopher exclaimed. Everyone was proud of Tommy's courage.

What would you do if you were caught in a storm?